CPS-MORRILL ES

3 24571 0902205 7   921 MIN
Nicki Minaj

W9-BJR-300

HIP-HOP

Biographies

NICKI MINAJ

SADDLEBACK
PUBLISHING

HIP-HOP Biographies

Chris Brown

Drake

50 Cent

Jay-Z

Nicki Minaj

Pitbull

Rihanna

Usher

Lil Wayne

Kanye West

SADDLEBACK
PUBLISHING
www.sdlback.com

Copyright © 2013 by Saddleback Educational Publishing. All rights reserved. No part of this book may be reproduced in any form or by any means, electronic or mechanical, including photocopying, recording, scanning, or by any information storage and retrieval system, without the written permission of the publisher. SADDLEBACK EDUCATIONAL PUBLISHING and any associated logos are trademarks and/or registered trademarks of Saddleback Educational Publishing.

ISBN-13: 978-1-62250-010-9
ISBN-10: 1-62250-010-5
eBook: 978-1-61247-691-9

Printed in Guangzhou, China
NOR/0413/CA21300571
17 16 15 14 13   2 3 4 5 6

Table of Contents

Timeline

1982: Onika Maraj born in Trinidad on December 8, 1982.

2000: Onika graduates from high school.

1987: Onika's parents leave her in Trinidad with her grandmother.

2005: Onika pays to record her own music and posts it on MySpace.

1989: Onika's parents take her to New York City.

2006: Fendi finds Onika's MySpace page. He asks her to perform on his DVDs.

Onika changes her stage name to Nicki Minaj.

1996: Onika is accepted into La Guardia High School for Music and Art

2007: Nicki meets Lil Wayne and starts releasing mixtapes of her music.

2009: Nicki Minaj signs recording contract with Lil Wayne's Young Money Entertainment.

2010: Nicki breaks *Billboard* record with seven singles on the Hot 100 chart at one time.

Nicki releases first album, *Pink Friday*, on November 19, 2010.

2011: Nicki performs on national television on *Saturday Night Live*. *Pink Friday* becomes the Billboard number-one selling album. Nicki wins two American Music Awards.

2012: Nicki is nominated for three Grammy Awards. Nicki performs with Madonna and M.I.A. at the Super Bowl halftime show. The album *Pink Friday: Roman Reloaded* is released. Nicki performs as Steffie in *Ice Age: Continental Drift*.

Tough Childhood

People find it very hard to describe Nicki Minaj. She is a very successful solo rap artist. But that leaves out her talent in other styles of music. You could describe her as a fierce feminist. But she also works hard at being really cute. Fans of Nicki Minaj understand that she is anything but simple.

Onika Tanya Maraj was born in Trinidad on December 8, 1982. Trinidad is a small island between North and South America. Onika's parents moved to New York when she was a toddler. Onika stayed in Trinidad with her grandmother and many cousins.

Onika grew up in her grandmother's small house in Trinidad.

Onika missed her parents so much. Every time her mother came to visit, the little girl would get dressed and pack her things. She would sit in her room and wait for her mother. Onika wanted to go to New York so her family could be together. She remembered, "I would sit there and wait for her to leave, knowing that if she sees that I'm dressed, she'll take me with her." But each time Onika's mother would go back to New York without her.

Her grandmother lived in a small house. It felt even smaller because so many people lived there. Onika was sure that her parents had a fancy home in the United States.

Onika's parents finally came for her when she was five years old. They would live together in New York City. She was so excited! But when she got to Queens, New York, she was disappointed. Not everyone in the United States was rich. Her home in New York was not the fancy house of her dreams.

Onika's parents were poor. Worse than that, her father was addicted to alcohol and crack. Her father could not keep a job because of his addictions. The crack he used cost money. So Onika's father would steal things from their home. He sold them to pay for his drugs.

The addiction led to danger. When Onika's father would drink or use drugs, he would hurt Onika's mother. He even threatened to kill her. Onika kept a diary for a while, but her father found it. She was afraid that he would be even more angry reading about what he was doing. To keep her mother safe, she stopped writing.

One day, Onika's father tried to kill her mother. He burned down their house. All of their belongings were destroyed. Onika was angry at her father for a long time. She rapped about it in her song "Autobiography." The words to her song described how hurt Onika was by her father's actions. She had nightmares in which her father killed her mother. She had trouble sleeping. Onika also did not understand why her father was not sent to jail.

Onika read a lot to avoid her family's troubles. "I don't know," she said. "In all the books I read, there were big houses, and they had all this nice stuff, and I always wished that could be my family." Onika wanted to grow up to have these things. If she made money, she could take care of her mother and brother.

Onika's father set their home on fire because he wanted to kill her mother.

Onika, her brother, and her mother were not hurt in the fire. Onika's mother wanted to keep them safe, so she hid them. She worked as a nursing assistant. She moved them to shelters when she needed help. When she had enough money, she rented an apartment. They moved often. Onika's mother hoped that Onika's father would not find them.

Onika remembered, "We moved so many times when I was a kid. We were always running away from him. Whenever we got to a new house, he would find us."

The family had lost their belongings in the fire. Onika's mother tried keeping her children's spirits up. She did not have the money to buy them things. But she could fill their lives with music. Onika recalled, "I knew the whole Diana Ross collection before I was eight."

Onika's mother left her husband, but she did not divorce him. She just hid from him. Finally, Onika's father went to rehab. He learned how to stop drinking and using drugs. He fought his addictions. He was able to control his temper and stop hurting people. Onika's mother saw him change. Slowly, she started letting him see her and their children.

Onika's parents started going to church. Then her parents got back together. Onika was not as quick to forgive her father. She still worried about her mother. She wanted her mother to be strong enough to care for herself and her kids. So Onika kept dreaming of becoming rich so she could care for everyone. She even told her family that she would be a soap opera actress. She wanted to be rich and famous.

Onika's mother shared great music with her children, such as the songs of Diana Ross and the Supremes.

Discovering Her Talents

Onika used her imagination a lot as a child. "Fantasy was my reality," she said. She pretended to be other people. Her favorite was a girl she called Cookie. She even got her friends to call her by this new name. She also liked music and writing poetry. In grade school, she played the clarinet. By the time she was twelve, her poetry and music came together. She started writing rap.

Onika went to her neighborhood public school through eighth grade. She had an opportunity to attend a magnet school when she reached high school. Magnet schools focus on special talents. New York City had magnet schools for very good science students. It had a school for students who wanted to become lawyers or police officers. It also had a school for students who loved performing arts. It was called Fiorello H. LaGuardia High School of Music and Art and Performing Arts. The school inspired the movie *Fame*. It also inspired Onika.

In order to get into LaGuardia, students had to audition. They could sing, play an instrument, or act. Onika did not play the clarinet well enough to get in playing an instrument. She was a good singer. That was how she planned on getting in to the school. On the day of the audition, her voice was hoarse. She sang in front of the judges. Her voice sounded terrible.

"I knew I'd flunked miserably," Onika said. "I was crying and embarrassed, and I didn't want anyone in the school to see me.

I just wanted to go home. That was the first time in my adolescent life where my mother put her foot down. Normally I made the rules." Onika's mother would not let her hide from her failure. Instead, she made Onika go back to the school. She made Onika audition for the acting program.

Onika pretended to be other characters around friends and family. But she had never acted for an audience before. She also never acted from someone else's script. She auditioned anyway and was accepted into LaGuardia. She recalled, "You know when you're doing something you were put here to do, and there's a moment when it's so easy. And you're like, 'Wait, not everyone can do this?'"

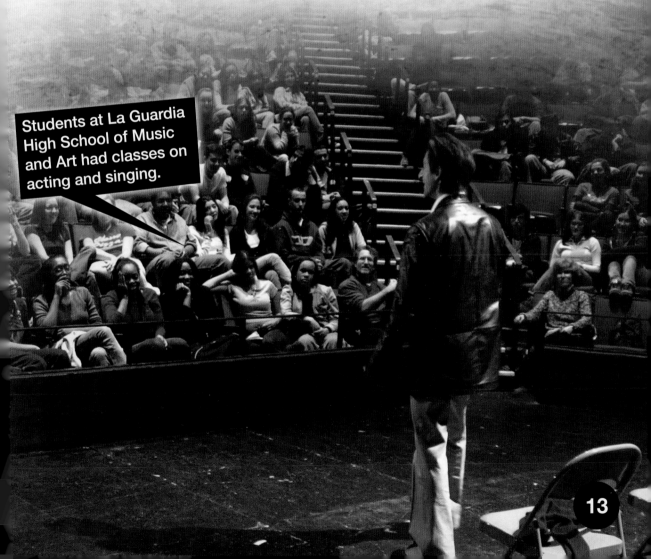

Students at La Guardia High School of Music and Art had classes on acting and singing.

When Onika graduated from high school, she did not go to college. She also did not try to get acting jobs. She wanted only two things: a BMW and time to record music. Both of these took money, so Onika got a job.

She worked as a waitress at a Red Lobster restaurant. She was not a great waitress, either. She liked wearing long, fake fingernails. They would pop off and land on her customers' plates.

Finally, she was fired. When a customer signed his receipt, he kept her pen. Onika chased him into the parking lot to yell at him. She was not mad that she lost her job. She was happy that she showed the customer and her boss that she was tough.

She waited tables at other restaurants. She took office jobs too. She was fired every time. But she made enough money for her fancy car. She also made enough to pay for time in a recording studio.

Onika loved to rap. She had a lot of male friends in Queens who were rappers. They wanted Onika to sing the background parts on their songs. Onika was not interested.

She said, "I hated doing anything that made me seem like a girl at that time. I wanted to be as strong as the boys and as talented as them, and I wanted to show them I could do what they did."

Onika would pay to record her own raps. She would put the CD of her song in her car. Then she would drive around Queens with her windows down so everyone could hear her music. People always turned their heads to listen.

Onika worked as a waitress to pay for a car and studio time.

In the early 2000s, there were some women in hip-hop. But there were many more male rappers than female rappers. Onika wanted to be a hip-hop star. So she paid close attention to the women who were succeeding.

Lil' Kim was a rapper from Brooklyn. She sold millions of records and topped the music charts. Onika loved Lil' Kim's sound and her toughness. Foxy Brown was from Brooklyn too. Her family moved to New York from Trinidad, just like Onika's. Some people put Brown down for swearing. She was not afraid to stand up for herself. She was arrested for fighting more than once. Onika did not fight like Brown did. But she liked Brown's tough attitude.

Missy Elliot was the queen MC. She was the only female rapper to have six platinum albums. She wrote her own music. Other hip-hop artists paid her to write their songs. She also helped launch the careers of other rappers, such as Ginuwine. Elliot also grew up with a violent father. Onika could relate to Elliot.

Onika wanted to be a successful female rapper like Missy Elliot.

Onika's most surprising influence was a singer from her tween years. Cyndi Lauper was not a rapper. Instead, she sang *pop* music. One of her biggest hits was the song "Girls Just Want to Have Fun." Lauper had many hit records starting in the early 1980s. Lauper was very well known for her hair and clothes. Onika said, "I love Cyndi Lauper's style. I remember watching her as a kid and thinking, 'I don't know who this is, but I want to hang out with her.' Her style looked like a piece of art to me." Onika used what she learned from Lauper to make her own style.

Onika was a huge fan of Cyndi Lauper's style.

Creating Characters

Onika started singing backup for New York City rappers. She was writing music for herself at the same time. She developed her first musical character, Harajuku Barbie. She would perform dressed as this character. You could not miss her pink, girlie style.

Onika then did something that changed her career. She set up a MySpace account. MySpace is a website where people can post messages, pictures, and music. It was the most popular social media website until Facebook came along.

People in the music business would look at MySpace pages to find new singers. That was how Onika was discovered. A producer named Fendi started Dirty Money Records in 1998. Fendi worked with Lil' Kim and other rap artists. He was listening to hip-hop artists on MySpace. He noticed Onika's page. Her beautiful pictures and powerful songs were just what he was looking for.

Fendi produced *The Come Up*. He called it a DVD magazine. He would feature one or two stars on the cover. Then he would put a couple of videos from the stars on the DVD. The rest of the DVD would be full of videos with new artists and good-looking women. Onika was both! Fendi put Onika's videos on many DVDs. One of them featured hit rapper Lil Wayne. Onika's work on that DVD caught Lil Wayne's attention.

The Come Up made Onika very popular. Fendi hoped to make Onika a star and get her signed to a major record company. He thought her name did not sound interesting enough. So he suggested she change her name to Nicki Minaj. She said, "I fought him tooth and nail. But he convinced me. I've always hated it."

Harajuku Barbie was Nicki's first musical character.

19

Lil Wayne liked Nicki Minaj's work on Fendi's DVDs. Lil Wayne had his own record label, Young Money. He offered Nicki a recording contract. He started out by making a mixtape to show off her style. The mixtape, *Playtime is Over*, came out in April 2007. It had a number of songs on it. Lil Wayne sent the mixtapes to DJs to play in clubs and at parties. The tapes got audiences excited and interested in Nicki's music.

Lil Wayne had Nicki singing on other mixtapes too. She sang with him, T.I., and Jeffree Star. Lil Wayne also sang on her mixtapes to make them more popular. With Lil Wayne's help, Nicki was becoming well-known. She performed with other Young Money rappers. She also had small concerts of her own.

At one point, Nicki nearly ruined her career. Lil Wayne was recording an album and asked Nicki to perform with him. She decided to go perform at a show instead of going to the recording studio. When Nicki did not show up at the recording studio, Lil Wayne fired her.

Nicki realized the mistake she made. She scrambled to make things right again. She wrote new verses just for him and asked to meet with him. She performed her verses for him. Lil Wayne made her wait, not giving her an answer. Finally, after making her very uncomfortable, he let her back in the record company.

For two years, Nicki worked very hard. She continued to sing backup for Young Money artists. Lil Wayne also helped her make two more mixtapes. Her music was getting national attention. She did not have an album out yet, but MTV was playing her songs.

Lil Wayne helped Nicki make mixtapes that made her very popular.

Nicki appeared at the 2011 Grammy Awards with Lil Wayne.

With Lil Wayne's help, Nicki developed her musical style. She created characters that she would act as while she rapped. She said, "I feel it's like one big theater piece. It's a show." Nicki explained, "I like playing dress up."

Harajuku Barbie was Nicki's first character. She has a high-pitched voice and a sweet personality. In honor of this character, Nicki calls her female fans Barbz and her male fans Ken Barbz.

Harajuku Barbie is the opposite of another character, Roman Zolanski. For this character, Nicki plays an angry man. She acts in ways that women are not usually expected to act. Nicki also acts as Roman's mother, Martha. She talks with a thick British accent. The character Rosa is Spanish, and Nicki Teresa can heal people.

To Onika, Nicki Minaj is a character too. Her family does not call her Nicki. That is the person who raps and performs on stage. At home, she is the same Onika that they knew growing up.

So how do fans know which character she is performing as? Nicki does not dress up much, and her hair is black. Roman may dress in crazy, out-of-this-world outfits. Barbie, of course, is in pink. Nicki Teresa has a scarf on her head. Martha and Rosa have accents, so fans can tell them apart by the way they talk and sing.

Why does Nicki use characters? She says, "I have a lot of freedom to be crazy. I can rap in a London accent, make weird faces, wear spandex, wigs, and black lipstick. I can be more creative than the average male rapper."

Becoming a Star

Nicki moved from being a background performer to a cameo artist. Her name was listed with the star on each recording. She stood out instead of blending in the background.

From 2008 to 2010, Nicki was asked to perform on over thirty different records. She learned her lesson when Lil Wayne fired her. She showed up for her recording sessions on time. She was prepared and professional. And she had a fierce rap. Nicki earned a great reputation as an MC. She made $50,000 when she rapped on someone else's song.

Nicki made *Billboard* magazine history before she ever had an album of her own. (*Billboard* tracks how well songs and albums sell.) Nicki had seven top-selling singles on *Billboard's* Hot 100 chart at one time. No other single singer had done this before. Nicki released the single "Your Love." In addition, she rapped on:

"My Chick Bad" by Ludacris

"Knockout" by Lil Wayne

"Bottoms Up" by Trey Songz

"Lil Freak" by Usher

"Letting Go (Dutty Love)" by Sean Kingston

"2012 (It Ain't The End)" by Jay Sean

Nicki won awards for Best Female Hip-Hop and Best New Artist at the annual BET Awards. She dedicated the award to Lil Wayne. She was also nominated for a Teen Choice Award, a People's Choice Award, and an MTV Video Music Award. Nicki was officially a star.

Then in November of 2010 she released her first album, *Pink Friday*. The first week the album was out, it was *Billboard's* number two selling album. It would become the top-selling album in the country in just a few weeks.

All of this success came before she released her first album!

Nicki was a top-selling performer before her first album was released.

Nicki knew she wanted a career as big as that of the male MCs. But she was very careful on *Pink Friday*. She did not curse much. Her songs were not too rude or too proud. This was very different from male rappers. They are often boastful and use strong language in their songs.

Nicki understood the business of hip-hop. Her songs could not include too much profanity if she wanted them played on the radio. Being played on the radio meant that more records sold. Artists who sold a lot of records got more freedom from their record companies. And Nicki wanted more freedom.

Pink Friday proved that Nicki could sell a lot of records. So she took on the proud, strong style that she wanted in her concerts. Some people criticized her new style. But she said that female rappers should get the same respect that male rappers do. Nobody asked rappers like Eminem or Lil Wayne to be nicer or more polite.

Nicki said, "When you're a girl, you have to be everything. You have to be dope at what you do, but you have to be super sweet, and you have to be sexy, and you have to be this, and you have to be that, and you have to be nice, and you have to—it's like, 'I can't be all of those things at once.'"

Rap artists understood that Nicki was serious about her music. Kanye West described her as "the scariest artist in the game." He also said that she could be the second-best rapper of all time. He thought only Eminem was better.

Nicki wanted to be able to perform and sell as well as male MCs.

Topping Charts in Style

Fans loved to copy Nicki's clothes and hair. But she was not always a style icon. In high school, she wore baggy clothes and no makeup. She met a girl one year ahead of her who was interested in fashion and makeup. They became best friends. Nicki remembered, "She lived like five minutes away from me. So I went over and she made my face up. And I looked in the mirror and I thought that I looked sooooo beautiful. I was like, 'Oh my God!' I did not want to take that makeup off! I never wanted to wash my face."

Her hair was another story. She was trying new hairstyles from the time she was nine years old. She would take ideas from Cyndi Lauper and make them her own. She first tried blonde hair when she was fourteen. The hair stylist did not want to bleach her hair at first. She wanted Nicki to prove that her mother would not be mad. But Nicki cried and begged until the stylist gave in.

When Nicki became a hip-hop star, people looked to her to see what to wear. She appeared in fashion magazines. Fans copied her clothes and hair. Top designers invited her to their fashion shows.

The top name in women's fashion, Anna Wintour, knew Nicki by name and noticed what she wore. Nicki described a note that she got from Anna after they went to the same fashion show. "I got an autographed photo from her the next day that said, 'We match!' I had on these, like, weird balls and craziness, and she had on this really sophisticated dress. But they both were orange."

Nicki and Anna Wintour are both fans of fashion.

Music from *Pink Friday* made the charts through the end of 2010 and into 2011. One of the hits off the album was a bit of a surprise. The people at Young Money Entertainment did not plan on making "Super Bass" a single. But Taylor Swift changed all that. She mentioned on Twitter and on radio interviews how much she loved the song. Taylor's words made people want to hear the rap. The buzz over the song continued. Selena Gomez posted a video of herself on YouTube. She was rapping along with "Super Bass." Eventually the song sold four million copies. It was the first time a female solo rapper sold that many copies of a single.

Taylor Swift helped make "Super Bass" a huge hit. She and Nicki became good friends.

Nicki's hard work paid off. She was nominated for two American Music Awards. She was so proud to get the nominations. Nicki said, "That's a big deal. I worked really hard on *Pink Friday*, and that's my baby!"

Nicki Minaj was a big winner on the night of the awards. She was named Favorite Artist. *Pink Friday* won for the Favorite Soul/R&B Album. She beat out her mentor Lil Wayne and Kanye West for both awards. Later she was nominated for a Grammy Award. She lost to Kanye.

Nicki wrapped up the year getting an award from *Billboard* magazine. They named her the "Rising Star" for 2011. She received the honor at the Women in Music event in New York City. The head of *Billboard* said, "Nicki Minaj has established herself as a force in hip-hop and pop music." He continued, "We look forward to seeing where she goes and what she does next."

Nicki was named the "Rising Star" of 2011.

Nicki was happy to keep recording and performing with other musicians. She surprised Taylor Swift fans at a concert after the American Music Awards. Nicki came on stage and sang "Super Bass" with Taylor. Nicki knew how important Taylor was to the success of the song. Later Nicki told *Billboard*, "I performed it with Taylor, and she's so cute—she's like a big bowl of ice cream!"

Nicki loved other singers' music and working with other women. She surprised fans by saying how much she liked Enya's songs. Enya is an Irish singer known for her pop and new-age music. Nicki said, "Who doesn't love Enya? Whenever I'm in a trying time, she is the calm in the middle of the storm. If I put her on, I'll be in this crazy peaceful state. I love her style."

Nicki was becoming more successful. At the same time, more people began to criticize her. They said that she was turning away from hip-hop. They did not like that she was singing with pop stars like Britney Spears or Taylor Swift. Nicki answered, "I never only did rap . . . That's what irritates me. People always want to talk about who I was, but I've always been singing, always been experimenting with pop music . . . There's nothing wrong with that. I'm just broadening my fan base. I think everyone should enjoy music."

Nicki also did not like how women musicians were expected to not like each other. She said, "People never want to see females shine. They want to keep you bobbed down and keep you in a box where all you do is fight." Nicki instead wanted to work with other female singers and show off each other's talents.

Nicki loves other artists' music. Here she performs with Britney Spears.

suggestions to make their work even better. Nicki remembered, "Madonna had me in the studio writing my rap, and she really listened to it and said, 'Hmmm, you know what, is there a way you can incorporate such and such and such?' And I really changed it, and she loved it."

The icing on the cake was performing the song at the 2012 Super Bowl. Madonna described the performance as "the greatest show on earth in the middle of the greatest show on earth." The game and halftime show are shown on television. It is usually the most-watched television show of the entire year. Around 110 million people watch the game and show each time. So this was Nicki's largest single audience ever.

Nicki sang with Madonna during the Super Bowl halftime show in 2012.

It is common for artists to *diss* each other in the hip-hop community. Sometimes rappers call each other out on records. Radio and television interviewers will ask about *feuds* between artists. They hope to stir things up. It gets more people watching and listening to their shows.

Nicki posed like Lil' Kim on one of her earliest mixtapes. Lil' Kim dissed Nicki in interviews and on Twitter. She claimed that Nicki copied her look and sound. And while Lil' Kim was popular, Nicki proved to be far more successful. Nicki sang about being the best. Lil' Kim said those *lyrics* were aimed at her. Lil' Kim answered back on stage and in interviews. Nicki became more famous, and Lil' Kim became more angry. Kim released a song, "Black Friday," the same week that Nicki's album *Pink Friday* came out. In the song, she called Nicki a "Lil' Kim wannabe."

Nicki did not think she needed to diss Lil' Kim back in songs. She knew that just being successful was answer enough. She said, "My diss record is my success rate, and how much I can charge to be somewhere for thirty minutes. That's my diss record. The fact that I can pay your mortgage for a year in thirty minutes. That's my diss record."

Nicki also wondered why it was okay for black artists to diss each other. She asked, "Why in the black community have we got to hate on each other? Gaga didn't on Madonna . . . We're helping each other." Nicki would focus on staying successful. This was her way of winning.

Lil' Kim accused Nicki of stealing her look and sound.

Nicki released *Pink Friday: Roman Reloaded* and topped the record charts again.

In 2012 Nicki released her second album, *Pink Friday: Roman Reloaded*. Nicki had much more freedom on this album. Her character, Roman Zolanski, appeared on a number of songs. She mixed in more dance songs along with her rap. And the lyrics were much more explicit. Some critics were very upset that Nicki used the language that she did. Many parents did not want their kids to hear Nicki sing about sex or use bad words. Companies even offered her money to make "clean" music.

Nicki felt that this was a double standard. Male rap artists do not have the same criticism. She asked, "Why do people ask me to lose swear words? Do people ask Eminem to lose swear words? Do they ask Lil Wayne to lose swear words? I used to see Eminem in concert, and people were bringing their little brother or whatever. Nobody stops them and says, 'Would you stop swearing, Eminem, for loads of money?' I don't get it; I don't get it."

Nicki also understood that people expect more from women rappers. There was no way she could do what every fan and critic wanted. She said, "On the one hand you have people saying, 'We want her to be hard and raunchy and explicit,' and on the other hand there's, 'Nicki Minaj, would you stop swearing for the children, please?' It's like, what d'you want me to be?"

Despite all of her critics, *Pink Friday: Roman Reloaded* landed in the number-one spot of album sales its very first week. She also went on her first concert tour in the summer of 2012.

Branching Out

Nicki also tried her hand in other areas. She was invited to audition for *Ice Age: Continental Drift*. She remembered, "The original role that I was up for I didn't get. So I said, 'Oh, OK, whatever.' I was really mad. And the next thing you know, they called me and they said, 'We wrote in a part just for you 'cause we really want you to be a part of this movie.'" Nicki played the new character Steffie.

Celebrities such as Justin Bieber, Taylor Swift, and Beyoncé have their own perfumes. Nicki wanted to get into the fragrance business too. Nicki said, "I designed this scent and bottle with my Barbz in mind; I know they will love it!"

It made sense for her to have her own makeup. MAC Cosmetics worked with her to make a "Pink 4 Friday" lipstick. The lipstick was only sold for four Fridays. It sold out each week in just minutes.

MAC was so happy with Nicki that they wanted to work with her again. They asked her to work with Ricky Martin on the 2012 VIVA GLAM campaign. The company made two items. Nicki and Ricky would appear in commercials for them. All of the money made on the sales of their products went to HIV/AIDS charities.

Then Pepsi called. They loved her song "Moment 4 Life" from *Pink Friday*. They asked Nicki to perform a version of it as part of a commercial. Pepsi has often used the hottest music stars in their commercials. Michael Jackson and Beyoncé starred in earlier commercials. Nicki was in great company. Her fans were excited to see her on television again.

In 2012 *American Idol* made a big announcement. Nicki would be one of the show's new judges.

Making animated movies and selling soft drinks made Nicki even more popular with a young audience. Hip-hop is not usually aimed at kids. Nicki's music was not written with kids in mind. She said, "I never thought I'd have young fans. Never."

In fact, Nicki does not approve of kids' listening to explicit lyrics. "I don't want children cursing. I'm very strict on my nieces and my little brother. They have to listen to clean versions of music. Even my music." So Nicki records different versions of her songs that do not use explicit lyrics or talk about sex. These are the songs that are used in commercials and on family-friendly radio stations. These are also the versions she sings on daytime talk shows, like "*Ellen*."

Nicki also understands that some people will see her as a role model. She tells her Barbz, "Stay in school, respect your body . . . don't depend on a man. I tell them that all the time." Nicki does not change her style. Instead, she encourages her young fans to slow down. She says, "I always give my young little lady bugs my most precious advice, which is to say to a child, 'Don't rush to grow up.' "

Young fans love Nicki's fashion and music. But they know very little about her personal life. That is her choice. She is very careful about giving interviews. Nicki does not share too much information. She will not talk about people she might be dating. Fans will not see pictures of her partying in gossip magazines. Nicki Minaj may be a star, but Onika Maraj is a very private person.

Nicki entertained her young fans at the Kids' Choice Awards.

Nicki has done a lot to help those in need. Mattel made a custom Barbie that looked like her. She auctioned it to raise money for Project Angel Food, which gets meals to people who are ill with AIDS. She teamed up with two computer stores to sell items on the Friday after Thanksgiving. Normally that day is called "Black Friday," but the companies called it "Pink Friday." Money from the sales was donated to breast cancer research. She also autographed items for auction to raise money for Japanese earthquake victims.

It is important to Nicki to support her fans too. She understands what it is like to feel different. She explains, "It's okay to be weird. And maybe your weird is my normal. Who's to say?" She has tried not to judge the way people live. Nicki does not like being labeled, so she tries not to label others, either. "The point is, everyone is not black and white," Nicki said. "There are so many shades in the middle, and you've got to let people feel comfortable . . . I just want to be me."

Today Nicki remembers her childhood. It was so hard for her mother to raise her children and protect herself. Depending on her father nearly got Nicki's mother killed. So Nicki believes that girls need to learn to depend on themselves. Her message to them is very clear. "I want to show little girls that the possibilities are endless. That's my goal." Nicki knows what she wants her legacy to be: "I hope that girls that come after me will remember that Nicki Minaj said, 'Get your business in order first and then do what you love to do.' "

Nicki encourages girls and young women to be strong and independent.

Vocabulary

addict	(verb)	to depend on a drug, alcohol, or other habit
assistant	(noun)	a helper
auction	(verb)	to sell to the highest bidder
audition	(verb)	to try out in front of judges
autobiography	(noun)	a life story written by the person it is about
Billboard	(noun)	magazine that covers the music industry
cameo	(noun)	appearing briefly
characters	(noun)	people in a story or the people that actors pretend
clarinet	(noun)	a musical instrument that is played by blowing in a mouthpiece and pressing keys
diss	(verb)	to insult or put down
double standard	(noun)	a different set of expectations or rules, such as rules for women but not men
explicit	(noun)	profane or sexual
feminist	(noun)	a person who supports equal rights for women
feud	(noun)	a fight that lasts over a long time
Grammy Award	(noun)	an award given to the best recording artists every year by The Recording Academy
hip-hop	(adjective or noun)	using strong beats and chanted words; music that uses strong beats and chanted words
icon	(noun)	a person who stands as a great example
inspire	(verb)	to motivate or spur on
legacy	(noun)	something left behind by a person after he or she is gone

lyrics	(noun)	words to a song
magnet school	(noun)	a school that attracts students that have similar talents
MC	(noun)	a rap artist, short for "master of ceremonies"or "microphone controller"
mixtape	(noun)	a CD of songs made without a record company
MySpace	(noun)	popular website that users use to post information, photos, and music
new age	(adjective)	relaxing, inspirational
nominate	(verb)	to suggest that someone might deserve an award
performing arts	(noun)	things that can be performed, such as instrumental music, singing, and acting
platinum	(adjective)	a record that has sold at least one million copies
pop	(adjective)	generally appealing; a watered-down version of rock
producer	(noun)	a person who raises money to create a song, a stage show, and so on
profanity	(noun)	swearing or other inappropriate language
rap	(adjective, verb, or noun)	spoken with rhythm; to speak with rhythm; music in which words are spoken in rhythm
rehab	(noun)	a long-term therapy that teaches people how to stop using drugs or alcohol
ruin	(verb)	destroy
script	(noun)	the words to a play or other performance
shelter	(noun)	a home where people can go for protection
single	(noun)	one song, usually from an album
social media	(noun)	websites and other tools people can use to communicate with groups

Photo Credits

AP Images: Charles Sykes/Associated Press pp. 4–5; Joan Leong/Associated press p. 16; Evan Agostini/Associated press p. 31; PR Newswire p. 41; Chris Pizzello/Associated press p. 43

Getty Images: Science PR/Oxford Scientific pp. 8–9; RB/Redferns pp. 10–11; Theo Wargo/WireImage p. 13; Terry Lott/Sony Music Archive p. 17; Eamonn McCormack/WireImage p. 19; NBCUniversal p. 21; Kevin Mazur/WireImage p. 22; Jeff Kravitz/FilmMagic p. 25; Kevin Winter/Getty Images Entertainment p. 27; Dimitrios Kambouris/WireImage p. 29; Lester Cohen/AMA2011/WireImage p. 30; Ethan Miller/Getty Images Entertainment p. 33; Kevin Mazur/WireImage p. 35; Andrew H. Walker/Getty Images Entertainment p. 37; Mark Davis/WireImage p. 38; John Parra/WireImage p. 45

Shutterstock: Kzenon p. 15.

Rex Features: Brian Rasic Cover; Jonathan Banks pp. 6–7.